YOU ARE LOVED

JENESSA WAIT

paige tate & co.

Published by Paige Tate & Co.
Paige Tate & Co. is an imprint of Blue Star Press
PO Box 8835, Bend, OR 97708
contact@paigetate.com
www.paigetate.com

Artwork by Jenessa Wait
Design by Megan Kesting

ISBN: 9781950968282

Printed in China

10 9 8 7 6 5 4 3 2

Hello! I'm Jenessa Wait, a Christian, wife, mom, and hand-lettering artist. My passion is to bring truth and encouragement to people's lives in a beautiful way.

I thank God every day for the gifts he has given me. I believe that He has given each of us a unique purpose in life and that when we receive His amazing strength, we can chase the dreams we were destined for. I created this book to share a collection of Bible verses and affirmations that have inspired me to live a more courageous, confident, and wholehearted life. I hope they can do the same for you.

No matter what season you are in right now, I want you to believe that you are loved and that you were chosen to be here for a reason. My prayer is that you will embrace this beautiful life and never doubt your value or your worth. I want you to cherish your identity as a daughter of the King, allow your creativity and talents to pour out, and let your light shine every step of the way. It is worth it. You are worth it.

WITH LOVE,

Jenessa

Each section of this book includes messages to help you breathe in joy, embrace the unknown, and honor the beauty and strength that God has given you in life. Read these pages in the morning, before bed, curled up with a cup of tea, or simply whenever you need a reminder that you are loved, chosen, and worthy.

Table of Contents

SECTION ONE

Believe in Yourself

EVERY DAY
YOU ARE
GROWING.

Today I will

1. FOCUS on the GOOD.
2. SEE my circumstances THROUGH the LENS of HOPE.
3. NOT WORRY
4. BELIEVE that miracles are POSSIBLE
5. TRUST God's plan!

NO ONE is YOU, that is your STRENGTH

REMEMBER TO BE
KIND TO YOURSELF IN
THE BECOMING, TO
CHAMPION EVERY
STEP OF VICTORY &
EMBRACE THE MOMENT
YOU ARE IN NOW.

GOD IS making a way

'And I myself will be a wall of fire around it,' declares the Lord, 'and I will be its glory within.'

-Zechariah 2:5

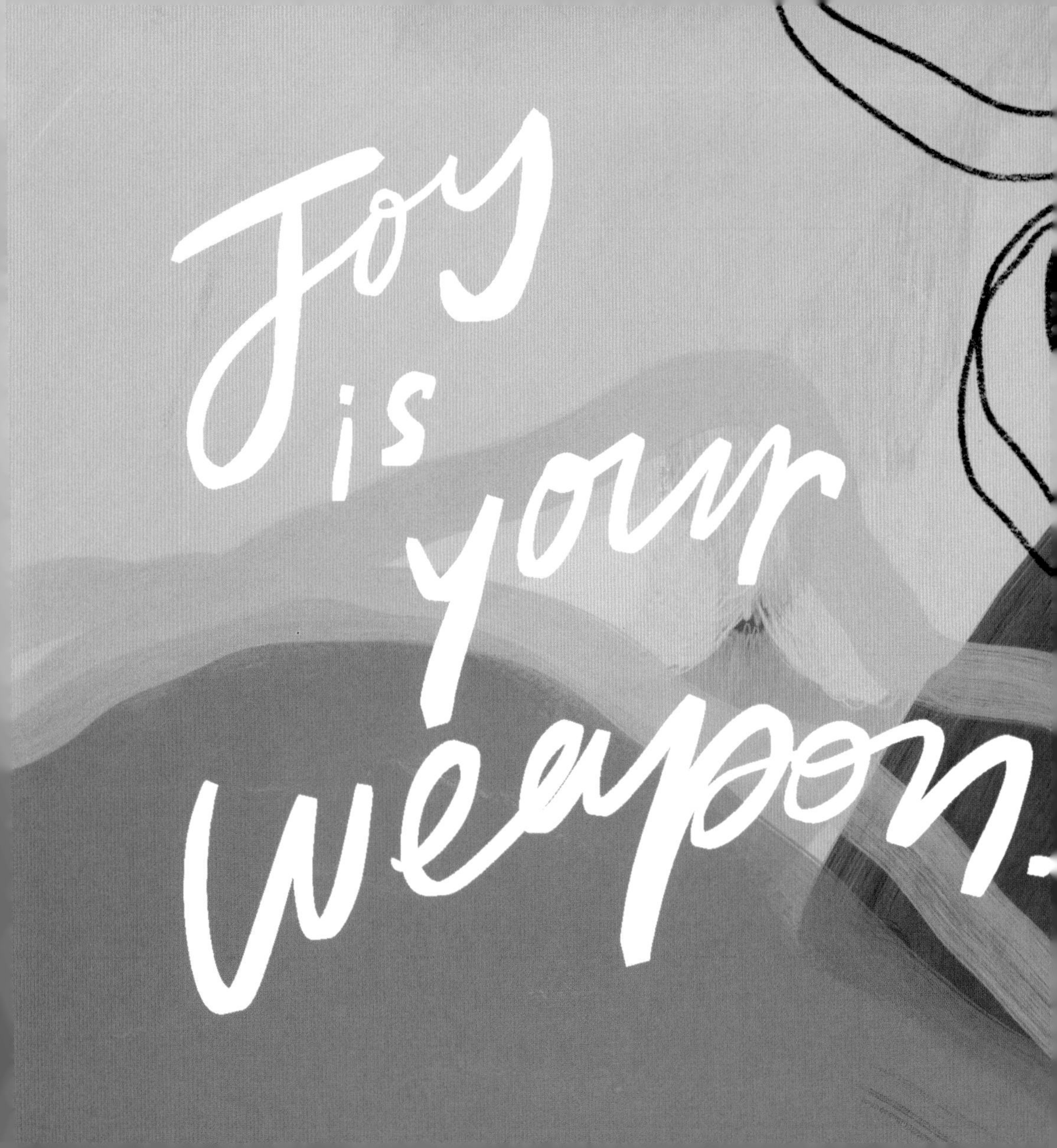
Joy is your weapon.

YOU ARE A TRAILBLAZER, A FORCE OF NATURE WHO IS MORE THAN CAPABLE TO DO WHAT YOU'RE CALLED TO DO.

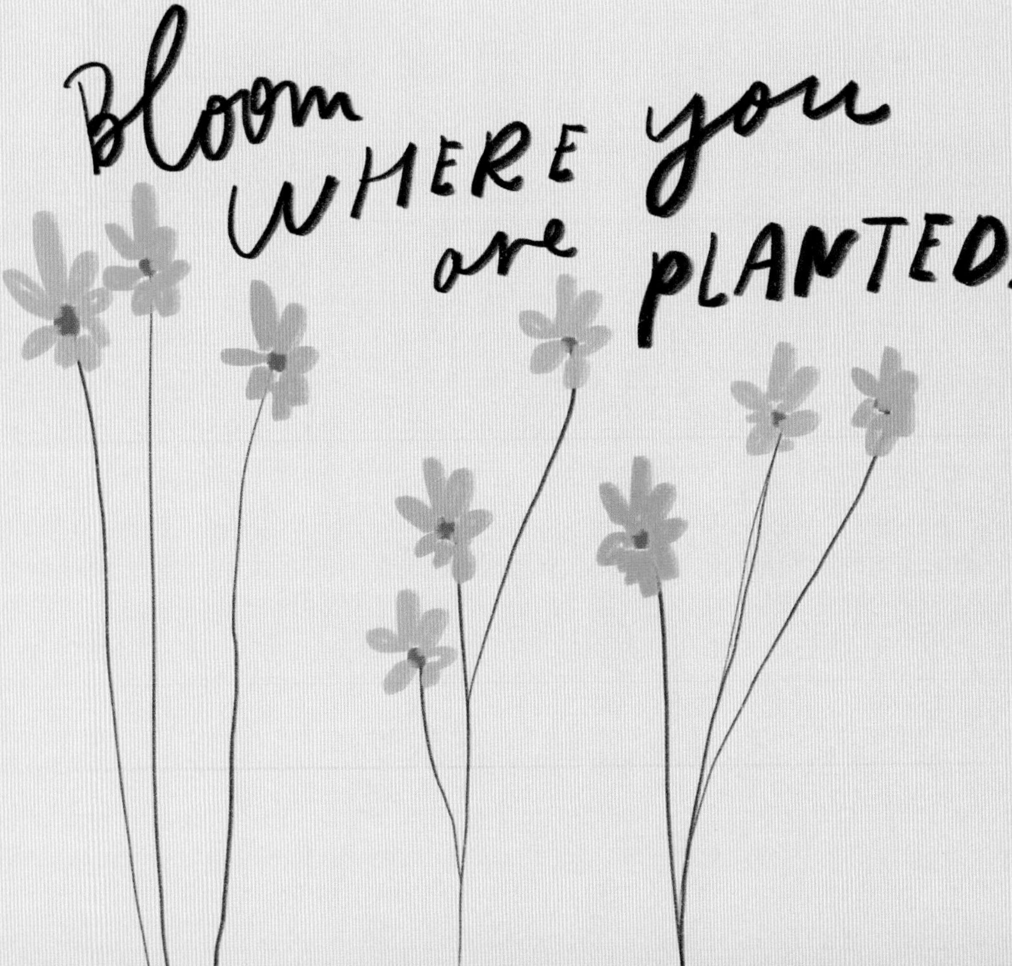
Bloom
WHERE you
are PLANTED.

Today I'm thankful for...

1) A GOD who is STEADFAST.

2) His MERCIES that ARE NEW every MORNING.

3) THE OPPORTUNITIES God has SET before me.

4) THE people God has put in my life to help me GROW.

5) COFFEE.

ALL THINGS

ARE POSSIBLE

Surely your goodness
& love will follow
me all the days of
my life, and I will
dwell in the house
of the LORD forever.

psalm 23:6

God is doing
a beautiful
work in you.
Trust the
process.

showing up fully today is one of the biggest keys in walking in the promises of tomorrow.

i will always
have hope.

NO MOUNTAIN IS TOO BIG
FOR YOU TO CONQUER. GOD HAS
PREPARED YOU FOR SUCH A TIME
AS THIS. KEEP YOUR HEAD UP.
HAVE CONFIDENCE & TRUST
THAT HE WILL GUIDE YOUR
EVERY STEP.

I AM A
DAUGHTER OF
THE KING,
SEATED IN
HEAVENLY
PLACES &
CAPABLE OF
MIGHTY THINGS.

Keep your eyes on Jesus

GOD WILL OPEN DOORS THAT NO MAN CAN SHUT.

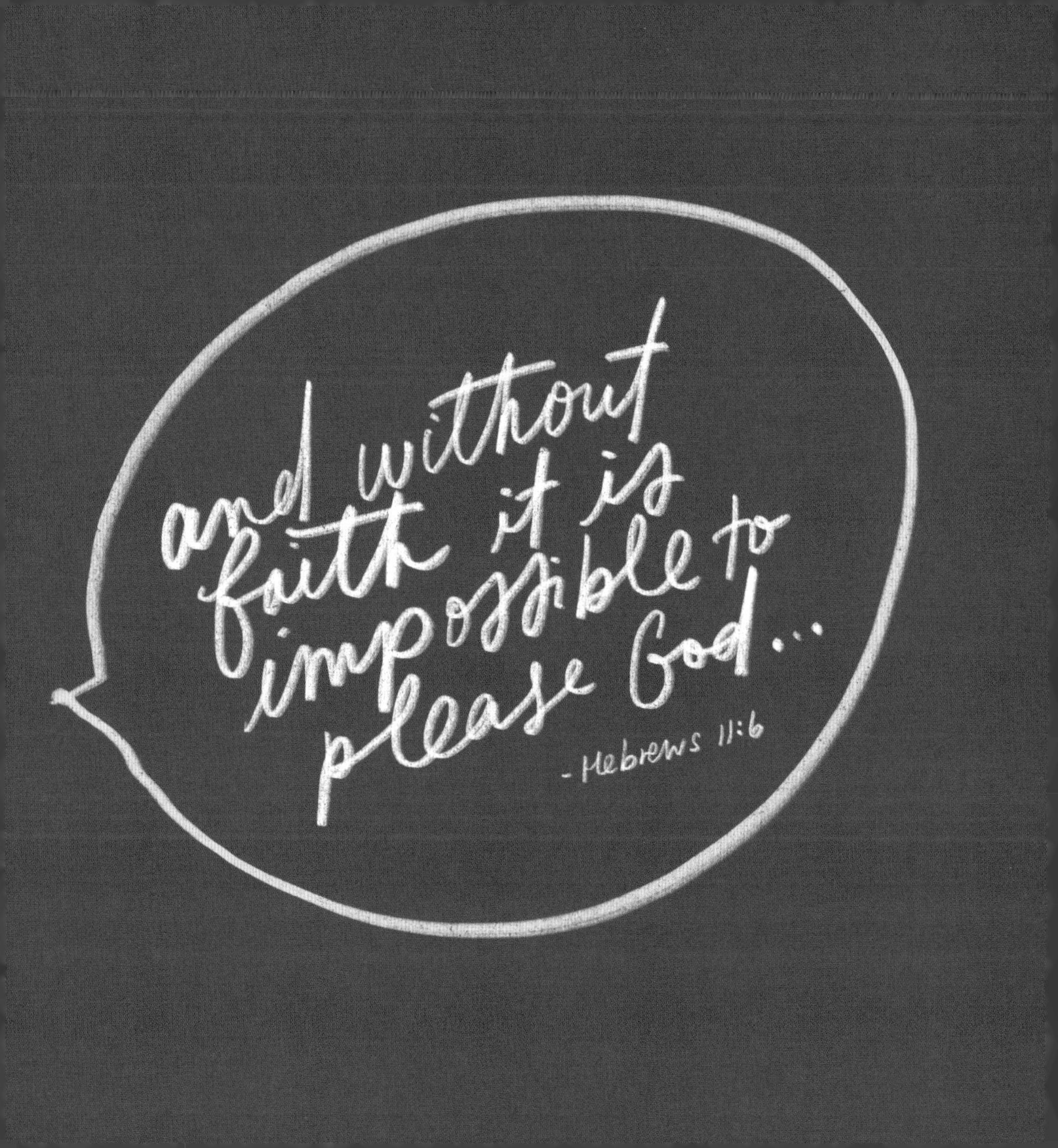
and without faith it is impossible to please God...
- Hebrews 11:6

SECTION TWO

Release your worries

God is merciful
God is merciful
God is merciful
God is merciful
God is merciful

Today I WILL:

1. LET GO OF WORRY.
2. BELIEVE THAT THE BEST IS YET TO COME.
3. HAVE FAITH IN A GOD WHO HOLDS TOMORROW.

God is for you
God is for you
God is for you
God is for you
God is for you
God is for you
God is for you
God is for you
God is for you

He will cover you with his feathers & under his wings you will find refuge.

Psalm 91:4

JUST KEEP MOVING FORWARD

YOU ARE NOT YOUR PAST. YOU ARE NOT YOUR MISTAKES. YOU ARE WHOLE, REDEEMED, + PURE. THAT'S WHO YOU ARE.

cling to HOPE!

NOTE TO SELF:

MY PRAYERS ARE
POWERFUL & ARE
MAKING AN IMPACT.
EVEN FAITH AS
SMALL AS A MUSTARD
SEED CAN MOVE
MOUNTAINS.

God's ability
to love you isn't
dependent on your
status, behavior,
or accomplishments.
It's a love that
always was,
always is, and
always will be.

HE IS YOUR
PRINCE OF
PEACE.

My grace is sufficient for you, for my power is made perfect in weakness.

- 2 Corinthians 12:9

EVEN IF I FAIL, TOMORROW I WILL TRY AGAIN.

3 Things to REMEMBER today

1. HIS MERCIES ARE NEW EVERY MORNING

2. GOD HAS NOT FORGOTTEN ABOUT THE PROMISES SPOKEN OVER MY LIFE.

3. I AM CHOSEN, I AM VALUABLE.

HIS PEACE
DWELLS
IN ME.

his goodness will follow you, all the days of your life

THE LORD IS MY SHEPHERD,
I LACK NOTHING.
PSALM 23:1

He restores to better than before
He restores to better than before
He restores to better than before
He restores to better than before
He restores to better than before
He restores to better than before

in every season I will praise Him

LOVE the LORD your GOD with all your heart and with all your soul and with all your mind and with all your STRENGTH.

Mark 12:30-31

my confidence is in Christ
my confidence is in Christ
my confidence is in Christ
my confidence is in Christ
my confidence is in Christ
my confidence is in Christ
my confidence is in Christ
my confidence is in Christ

SECTION THREE

Live life
in Wonder

Be the reason someone believes in miracles.

HE'S THE GOD WHO made
the STARS & THE
MOON, yet
HE still KNOWS
me BY NAME.

...let your light SHINE before others, that may see your GOOD DEEDS & glorify your FATHER in HEAVEN.

-Matthew 5:16

awaken
my
soul

I WILL PRAISE HIM IN THE VALLE
I WILL PRAISE HIM ON THE MOUNTAINTOP

JUST BE WHO
GOD CREATED
YOU TO BE.

5 THINGS TO REMEMBER

↓

1. NEVER LOSE YOUR awe & wonder.

2. GO OUT OF your way for somebody!

3. SAY 3 THINGS you LOVE about yourself.

4. NEVER have OFFENSE IN YOUR heart.

5. CHOOSE Joy.

CREATE
SOMETHING
BEAUTIFUL
TODAY-

DON'T TAKE LIFE TOO SERIOUSLY.

Enjoy it to the fullest!

HER HEART WAS
KIND & THE
WORLD WAS
MORE BEAUTIFUL
BECAUSE OF IT

START
EVERY DAY
WITH A
GRATEFUL
HEART.

TODAY IS A NEW DAY, WITH NEW MERCIES, BLESSINGS, & OPPORTUNITIES!

HE'S THE GOD OF Miracles.

Today is a GOOD Day TO Have a good Day!

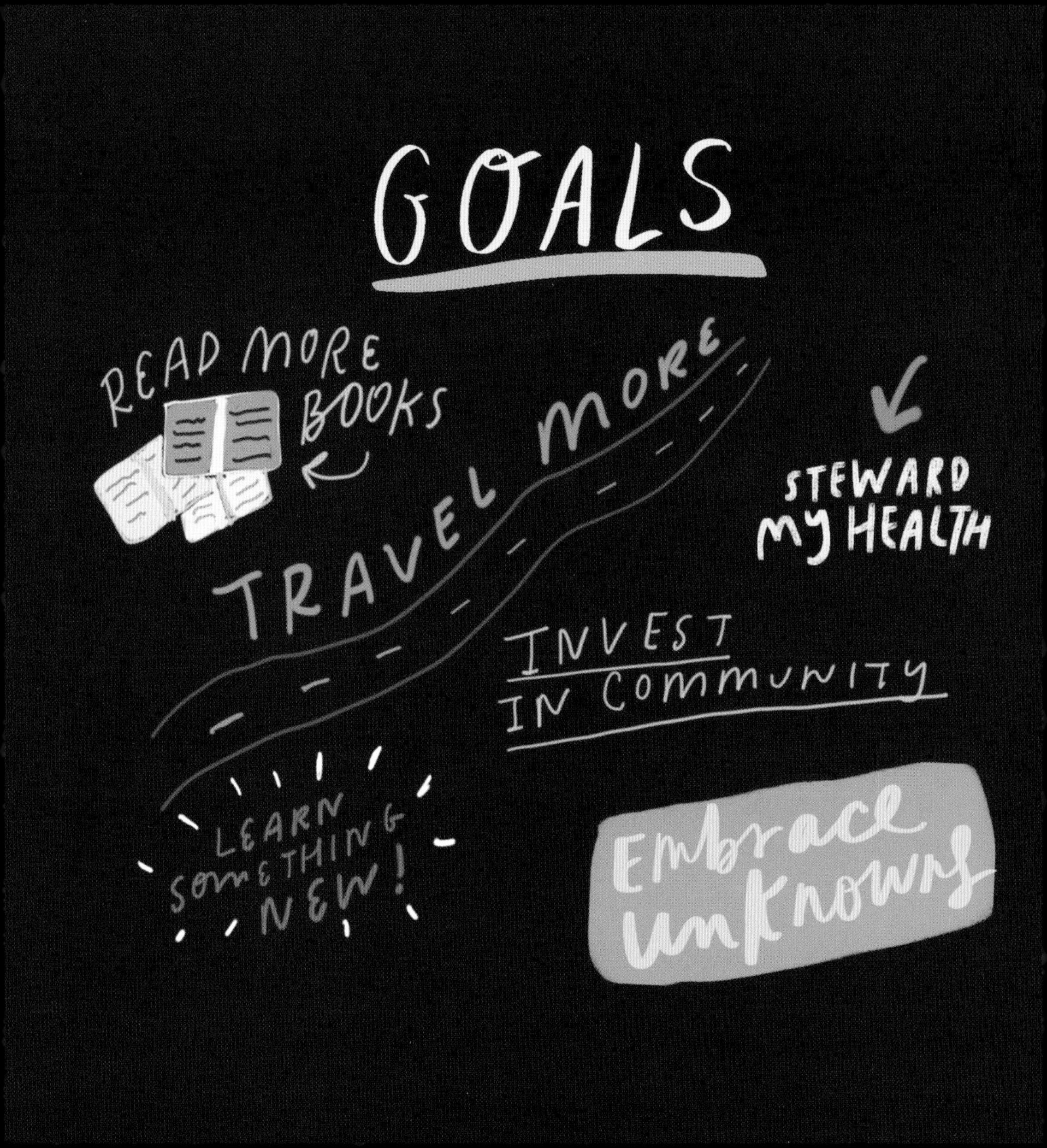
GOALS
READ MORE BOOKS
TRAVEL MORE
STEWARD MY HEALTH
INVEST IN COMMUNITY
LEARN SOMETHING NEW!
Embrace unknowns

today is your day of Victory

SECTION FOUR

Spread Kindness

INSTEAD OF ↓	TRY ↓
JEALOUSY	CELEBRATING
ISOLATION	VULNERABILITY
WORRY	TRUSTING
COMPLAINING	THANKFULNESS

TODAY I CHOOSE TO LIVE FROM LOVE, NOT FOR LOVE.

be quick to forgive, love unconditionally, and believe the best in everyone.

ON
EARTH AS
IT IS
IN
heaven

Matthew 6:10

Abide
IN HIS
love.

We are more than conquerors through him who loved us.

-Romans 8:37

LOVE BOLDLY WITH NO AGENDA, WITHOUT EXPECTING ANYTHING IN RETURN. LOVE FOR THE SAKE OF LOVE.

love
them
anyway

Be the reason that *someone* believes that God is really good.

THERE IS POWER IN MY HALLELUJAH.

THEREFORE I TELL YOU, WHATEVER YOU ASK FOR IN PRAYER, BELIEVE THAT YOU HAVE RECEIVED IT, AND IT WILL BE YOURS.

MARK 11:24

WE ALL HAVE A SEAT AT HIS TABLE

Today I'm THANKFUL FOR...

1) The BREATH in my LUNGS.
2) The people in my life who BELIEVE IN me.
3) A GOD WHO IS FOR me!
4) The grace to do what I'm called to do.
5) The JOURNEY that's brought me here.

THE LOVE OF
JESUS HEALS,
THE LOVE OF
JESUS RESTORES

Greater love has no
one than this: to
lay down one's life
for one's friends.

John 15:13

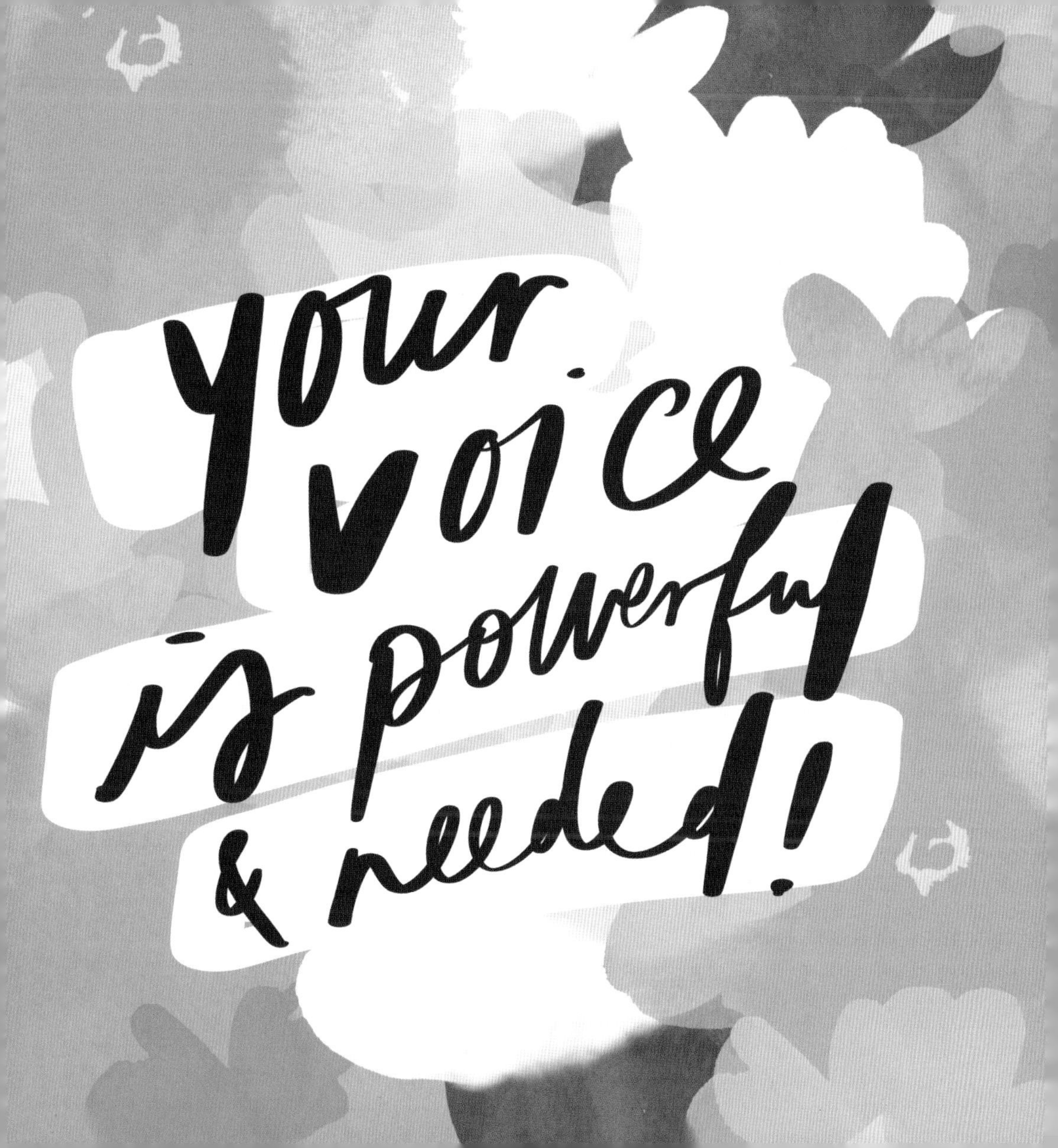
your voice is powerful & needed!

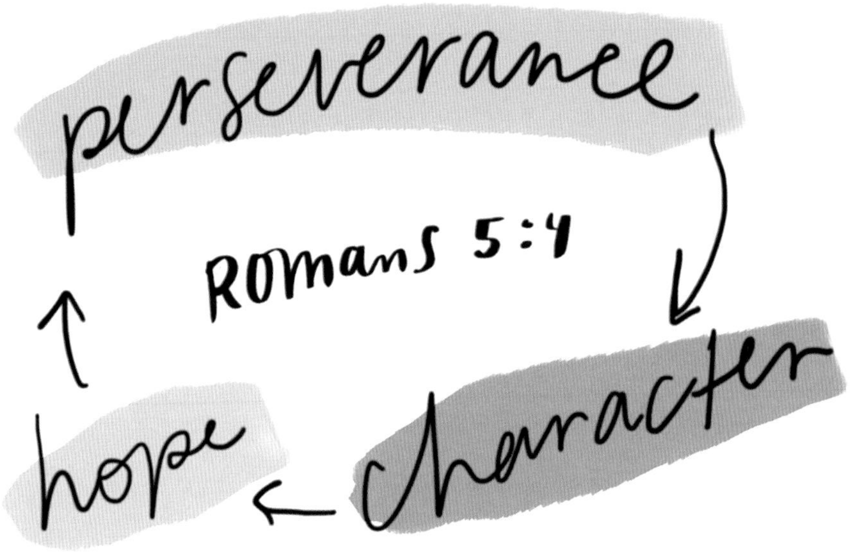
perseverance
Romans 5:4
character
hope

TODAY I WILL:

1. SHOW SOMEONE KINDNESS

2. THINK OUTSIDE THE BOX

3. SEE THE BEST IN OTHERS

4. CHOOSE TO HAVE HOPE

5. MAKE THE MOST OF TODAY

SECTION FIVE

Practice
patience

5 THINGS TO Remember

1. The LORD is for me and NOT against me
2. The LORD is my provider
3. Nothing is impossible for God
4. My future is in God's hands
5. God is with me in every season of life

your miracle is coming

EVEN IF YOU ONLY TAKE ONE STEP FORWARD TODAY, IT IS STILL CONSIDERED PROGRESS.

GOD ALWAYS has a plan.

HE GIVES ME A
HOPE AND A
FUTURE.

SPENDING TIME WITH GOD WILL...

1) CLARIFY YOUR PERSPECTIVE.
2) BRING PEACE OF MIND.
3) BRING FRESH HOPE.
4) RESTORE JOY.
5) REMIND YOU OF YOUR PURPOSE.

SHE NEVER STOPPED BELIEVING & SHE ALWAYS HAD HOPE.

there is beauty in the waiting

HE is FAITHFUL
in EVERY season.

THE WORLD NEEDS WHAT YOU CARRY.

LOVE IS PATIENT, LOVE IS KIND, IT DOES NOT ENVY, IT DOES NOT BOAST, IT IS NOT PROUD. IT DOES NOT DISHONOR OTHERS, IT IS NOT SELF-SEEKING, IT IS NOT EASILY ANGERED, IT KEEPS NO RECORDS OF WRONGS. LOVE DOES NOT DELIGHT IN EVIL BUT REJOICES WITH THE TRUTH.

— 1 CORINTHIANS 13:4-6

A LOVE SO DEEP IT CHANGES ME.

His will > My plans

The LORD bless you and keep you;
the LORD make His face shine on you and be gracious to you;
THE LORD turn His face TOWARD you AND give you PEACE.
—NUMBERS 6:24–26

my FUTURE is in GOD's hands.

She is UNSTOPPABLE, a *Loving* FORCE THAT will GREET YOU with kindness and grace. Wherever SHE GOES, BLESSINGS FOLLOW HER.

3 THINGS TO REMEMBER TODAY...

1. SLOW DOWN AND DON'T RUSH. ENJOY THE LITTLE THINGS.

2. TAKE A BREAK TO GIVE THANKS. WRITE OUT A LIST OF WHAT YOU'RE GRATEFUL FOR

3. GIVE SOMEONE A COMPLIMENT TODAY. SHOW KINDNESS BY AFFIRMING THE PEOPLE AROUND YOU!

Healthy things grow.

great
things
take time.

TAKE
DELIGHT IN
THE LORD
& HE WILL
GIVE YOU THE
DESIRES OF
YOUR HEART.

PSALM 37:4

grace will take you places that hustling never will

HOPE
HOPE
HOPE

SECTION SIX

Be
Fearless

LOVED

CHOSEN

ACCEPTED

VALUED.

YOU WERE NOT created to LIVE A COMFORTABLE life. YOU WERE BORN to BE an influencer & A RADICAL WORLD changer. Don't SHRINK back from the call God HAS for you! step into IT.

FEAR IS A LIAR

TRUST in the
LORD + LEAN NOT
ON YOUR
OWN
UNDERSTANDING.

TODAY I WILL
GIVE MY BEST
& BELIEVE THAT
GOD HAS MY BACK.
I WILL CHOOSE
FAITH OVER FEAR
& WILL CLING TO
HOPE NO MATTER
—WHAT.—

YOU ARE

enough.

if you're only talking to God about spiritual things, then you're missing out on a lot of good conversation it's time to run after every dream in your heart

I AM NOT A SLAVE TO FEAR.

I AM SAFE IN THE HANDS OF MY FATHER.

EVERYTHING WILL BE OKAY!

YOU ARE
WHAT YOU
BELIEVE
YOU ARE.

if you have faith as small as a mustard seed, you can say to this mountain, 'Move from here to there,' and it will move. Nothing will be impossible for you.
–matthew 17:20

you are free.

FOR OUR LIGHT
AND MOMENTARY
TROUBLES ARE
ACHIEVING FOR
US AN ETERNAL
GLORY THAT FAR
OUTWEIGHS
THEM ALL.

2 CORINTHIANS 4:17

faith > fear

IS ANYTHING
TOO HARD
FOR THE LORD?

- GENESIS 18:14

YOU ARE BRAVER
THAN YOU KNOW.

SECTION seven

Love Yourself
as you are

Be strong
& take
heart.

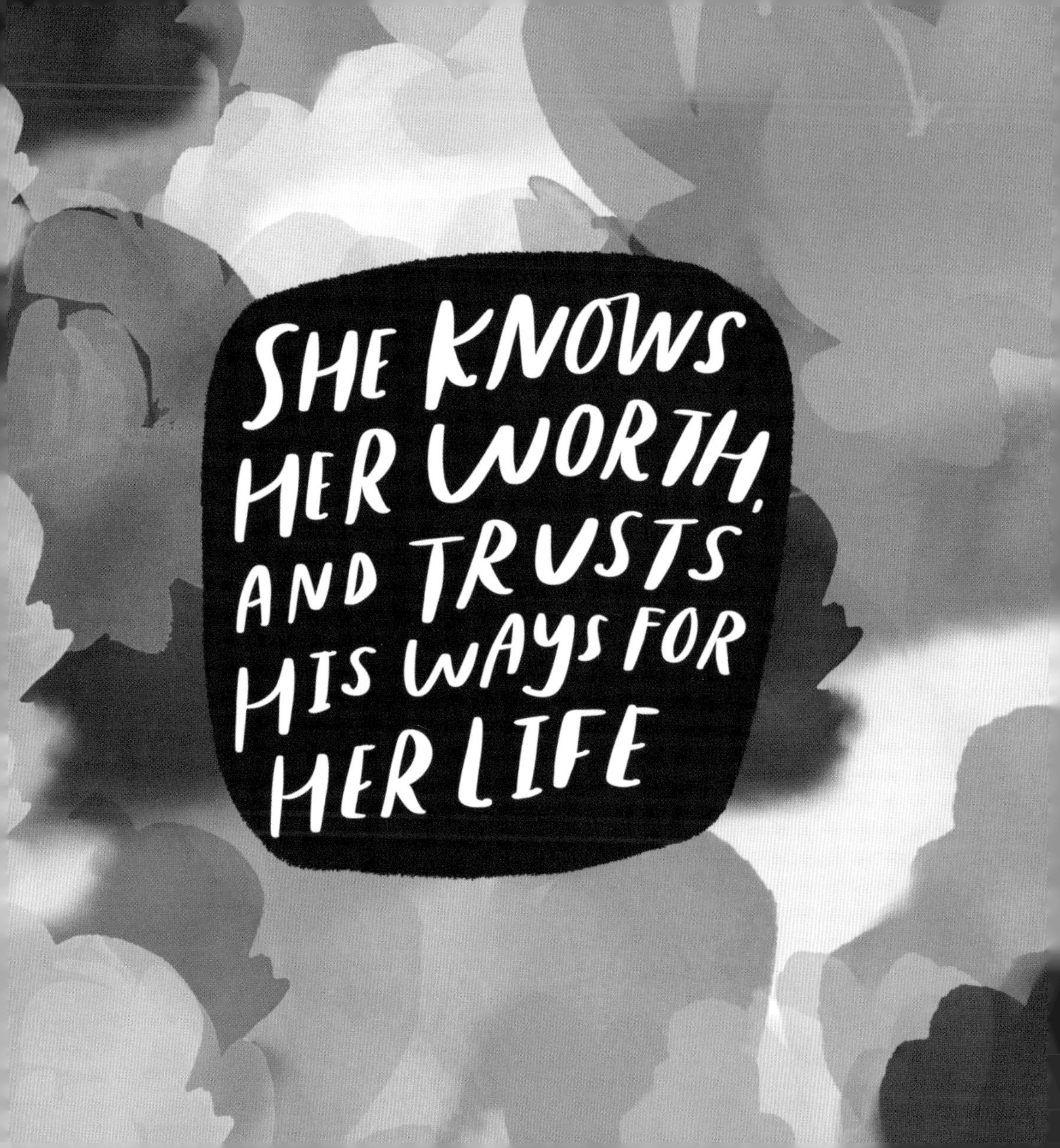
SHE KNOWS HER WORTH, AND TRUSTS HIS WAYS FOR HER LIFE

FOR THE SPIRIT
GOD GAVE US
DOES NOT MAKE US
TIMID, BUT GIVES
US POWER, LOVE,
& SELF-DISCIPLINE

–2 TIMOTHY 1:7

Let God love you as you are.

NOTE TO SELF:

THE WORLD NEEDS YOU
TO SHOW UP TODAY.
YOU ARE POWERFUL,
YOU ARE VALUABLE,
+ WHAT YOU BELIEVE
CHANGES THE WORLD.

she's beautiful,
she's worthy

lean into grace

GIVE THANKS TO
THE LORD, FOR HE IS
GOOD; HIS LOVE ENDURES
FOREVER - PSALM 118:1

PERHAPS THIS MOUNTAIN ISN'T TO *point* *at* YOUR WEAKNESS, *but* TO *SHOW* *you your* STRENGTH.

YOU
ARE
VALUABLE.

AND THEN SHE
REALIZED THAT
GOD WAS NEVER
AFTER HER PERFECTION
BUT RATHER
HER SURRENDER.

YOU ARE
GOD'S BEAUTY
ON
DISPLAY

5 keys TO A fruitful life

1) carry NO offense in your heart.

2) celebrate OTHER people's
↳ VICTORIES.

3) Know that YOU are LOVED not because of what you do, but because of WHO YOU ARE.

4) Don't allow fear or control to rule your life.

5) Pursue Jesus in all

bloom.

don't settle for good
when God has best
for you.

SEEK
FIRST
THE
KINGDOM.

you are doing
a good job

your life is
a beautiful
story, a story
of overcoming
that sings
a song of
redemption

God is Good.

I praise you because I am fearfully & wonderfully made; your works are wonderful, I know that full well

– PSALM 139:14

About the Author

Jenessa Wait is a Christian, wife, mom, and professional hand-lettering artist who believes that encouragement and truth have the power to change the way we live. She started her hand-lettering journey in 2015 as a hobby and it quickly turned into a thriving and successful online business selling journals, art prints, and home decor. Jenessa also teaches online courses and has partnered with brands like Causebox. When she's not creating, she and her husband serve as young adult pastors at Bethel Church in Austin, TX, where they reside.